Katherine Johnson

by Thea Feldman

illustrated by Alyssa Petersen

Ready-to-Read

Simon Spotlight

New York   London   Toronto   Sydney   New Delhi

SIMON SPOTLIGHT
An imprint of Simon & Schuster Children's Publishing Division
1230 Avenue of the Americas, New York, New York 10020
This Simon Spotlight edition July 2017
Text copyright © 2017 by Simon & Schuster, Inc.
Illustrations copyright © 2017 by Alyssa Petersen
All rights reserved, including the right of reproduction in whole or in part in any form.
SIMON SPOTLIGHT, READY-TO-READ, and colophon are registered trademarks of Simon & Schuster, Inc.
For information about special discounts for bulk purchases, please contact Simon & Schuster
Special Sales at 1-866-506-1949 or business@simonandschuster.com.
Manufactured in the United States of America 0617 LAK
2 4 6 8 10 9 7 5 3 1
This book has been cataloged with the Library of Congress.
ISBN 978-1-5344-0341-3 (hc)
ISBN 978-1-5344-0340-6 (pbk)
ISBN 978-1-5344-0342-0 (eBook)

CONTENTS

Introduction

What is your favorite subject in school? Have you ever thought about why you like it so much? Have you ever wondered what kind of a career you might have someday that involves your favorite subject?

You should meet Katherine Johnson.

From the time she was a very little girl, Katherine loved math. And she knew why, too. "It was hard," she said, remembering doing math in school, "but when you got it, you got it. You had to work for it. There was a right and a wrong, and you knew when you got there."

Another thing Katherine knew was that she would someday find a job that involved math. But even she never imagined that her math skills would help the US put the first man on the moon!

Chapter 1
A Family to Count On

On August 26, 1918, Katherine Johnson was born in White Sulphur Springs, West Virginia. She was the youngest of four children. Her father owned a farm, and her mother had been a teacher.

Ever since she could remember, Katherine was interested in learning—about almost anything! She couldn't wait to be old enough to start elementary school. Before then, she followed her siblings to school and tried to go in with them!

Most of all, Katherine loved to count. She counted family members, dishes, the number of steps from home to school, and so much more. "Everything is math!" Katherine said.

Katherine believed she got her gift for numbers from her father.

Even though her father had only completed the sixth grade, Katherine said he was the smartest man she ever knew. "He could look at a tree and know how many boards of wood he could get out of it," she said. He could solve any math problem too.

Before she turned six, Katherine finally started school. Because she could already read, she skipped first grade. She would skip fifth grade too. In school Katherine always had her hand in the air to ask questions. Her teachers encouraged her.

Each night Katherine and her siblings did their homework seated around a big table. "After I finished mine, I'd help them with theirs!" she recalled.

When Katherine was a little girl, most African Americans did not go to school beyond eighth grade. They went to work to help their families. At the time, the country also had a history of racial segregation. That means that there were many separate things for African Americans and white Americans, including schools. Katherine's hometown did not even have a high school for African Americans.

Katherine's father, however, was determined that all of his children would go to high school and to college, too. When Katherine's eldest brother, Charles, was ready for high school, Katherine's father moved the entire family one hundred and twenty miles away to Institute, West Virginia.

Institute had a high school for African Americans, and Katherine's mother and father made sure all their children graduated from it.

Katherine's parents

Katherine, her siblings, and her mother spent each school year in the town of Institute. Katherine's father stayed in White Sulphur Springs to take care of the farm. Because Katherine had skipped two grades, she started high school when she was just ten. She became a college freshman at fifteen. Most people start college when they are around eighteen years old!

Chapter 2
Math, Katherine's Number One Love

Katherine found it very exciting to be a student at West Virginia State College. There seemed to be countless classes she wanted to take! She especially loved French and thought she wanted to graduate with a degree in French, but she still loved math, too!

Then one day she ran into Mrs. Lacey, a math teacher she knew from back home. Mrs. Lacey insisted that Katherine sign up for her class. Mrs. Lacey made Katherine realize she wanted to concentrate on her math skills and graduate with a degree in math.

"I was just as fascinated with college math as I had been with high school math," Katherine remembered. She decided to major in math *and* French!

Katherine took every single math class the college offered. One of her other math professors, W. W. Schieffelin Claytor, even created a couple of new classes just for her! He told Katherine, "You would make a good research mathematician."

Katherine asked him, "What does a research mathematician do?"

Mr. Claytor answered, "You do research in mathematics!" (**Research** means to study materials in order to confirm facts and research new conclusions.)

Katherine asked, "Well, where do you get a job doing that?"

His reply was, "That's going to be *your* problem. But I am going to have you ready!"

Katherine *was* ready by the time she graduated with honors in 1937 at the age of eighteen. It was difficult at this time, however, for many African Americans, especially women, to find good jobs. The only good jobs for college-educated African American women at the time were teaching or nursing jobs.

After a few months Katherine got her first job. She taught French and piano to elementary school children. At her father's urging she went to graduate school too. During this time Katherine also got married

and started a family of her own.

In 1952 Katherine heard that the National Advisory Committee for Aeronautics (NACA), a government agency in Newport News, Virginia, was hiring African American female research mathematicians! Within a week she and her family moved to Newport News.

Katherine immediately applied for a job at NACA. She found out that all the jobs for the coming year had already been filled. So Katherine became a substitute teacher and did other work too. Then, the following year, NACA offered her a job!

Katherine was thrilled. She was finally going to find out what a research mathematician did.

Chapter 3
A "Computer" in a Skirt

Katherine started at NACA in June 1953. The agency was dedicated to flight research. Among other things, NACA engineers had developed the first aircraft that could fly faster than the speed of sound.

NACA's research work required a lot of complex math. In 1953, electronic computers were not generally used, so research mathematicians, who were often called "computers," did the math that the engineers needed.

Katherine joined a group of about twelve African American women who were research mathematicians. There was also a group of white American women research mathematicians. The two groups worked and ate separately until the Civil Rights Movement that had started in the 1950s brought an end to racial segregation in 1964.

At NACA, Katherine was finally able to see firsthand what a research mathematician did—and she loved it! "You had big data sheets, with maybe fifteen or twenty columns across and twenty-five lines down," she explained, "and you solved those all the way across for days. It was fascinating!"

Research mathematicians sometimes left the group and worked full-time with engineers on a specific project. When the project was done, they returned to the group. Shortly after she arrived, Katherine was sent to work full-time on a flight research project. The engineers quickly became impressed by Katherine's math skills, as well as her interest in learning as much about the project as she could.

Working on the project, Katherine did what she always did: She asked a lot of questions! She knew that the more she understood about the project, the better her contribution to it would be.

"There is no such thing as a dumb question," Katherine always said. "It's dumb if you don't ask it." Because of her intelligence, curiosity, and upbeat attitude, Katherine never returned to the group of research mathematicans. She was requested on many special projects.

Katherine was a valued member of NACA when the agency turned its focus to space exploration in the late 1950s. The United States and the Soviet Union were then the two most powerful countries  in the world. (The Soviet Union was a former federation of Communist republics occupying the northern half of Asia and part of Eastern Europe. Its capital and largest city was Moscow.) However, each wanted to be number one, and that included being the first nation to explore space. In 1958, NACA became the National Aeronautics and Space Administration, or NASA. Its efforts became devoted to what was called the "Space Race."

Little did Katherine know at the time just how far she, NASA, the US, and the entire world would go!

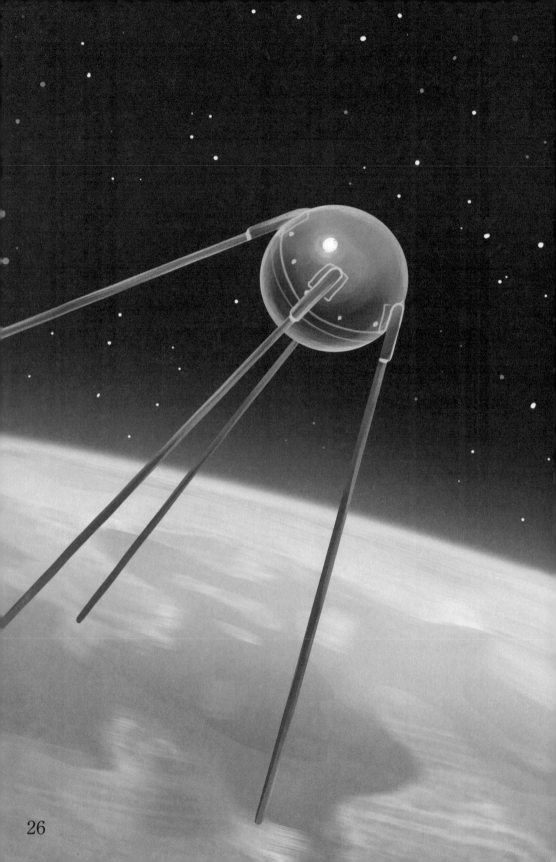

Chapter 4
Katherine Takes Off!

The Soviet Union took an early lead in the Space Race. In 1957 they launched *Sputnik 1*. It was the first man-made satellite to successfully orbit the Earth. (A **satellite** is a small object that revolves around a larger object.) The US launched its first satellite the following year.

The Soviet Union took the lead again when it came to sending a man into space. On April 12, 1961, cosmonaut Yuri Gargarin (a Russian astronaut is called a **cosmonaut**) orbited the Earth aboard *Vostok 1*. The US followed less than a month later. On May 5, 1961, astronaut Alan Shepard made a partial orbit around the Earth in *Freedom 7*.

It had required extremely complex and precise mathematical calculations to arrive at the proper flight path for the spacecraft and to keep Shepard safe. Who had done the math? Katherine!

For her entire career Katherine insisted that no one person was responsible for any specific achievement. She believed in teamwork. However, she also knew just how skilled she was at math. NASA knew it too!

NASA put Katherine on the team that worked to send *Friendship 7* and astronaut John Glenn into space on February 20, 1962. Katherine worked on the tracking system that would predict, within two miles, where the spacecraft would land after making three full orbits around the Earth.

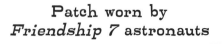

Patch worn by
Friendship 7 astronauts

NASA was relying on its first electronic computer to calculate *Friendship 7*'s flight path. John Glenn, however, had more faith in Katherine than in any new technology. He insisted that Katherine check the computer's numbers! He said, "If she says the computer is right, I'll take it."

Katherine worked for a day and a half on the calculations that the computer had done. She arrived at the same exact numbers!

Katherine's precise spaceflight calculations were not her only unique accomplishments at NASA. Early in NASA's history, only men attended the briefing meetings where spaceflight was discussed. Katherine wanted to be at those meetings and kept asking if she could go. She even asked, "Is there a law against it?"

Katherine's persistence paid off. She was eventually invited to attend all briefing meetings, and she participated in the discussions. She was also the first woman in her division to have her name included on a report. The report contained theories Katherine had helped to develop about how to launch, track, and bring back spacecraft.

Katherine also became an important member of the team behind *Apollo 11*.

By the late 1960s both the Soviet Union and the US had landed unmanned vehicles on the moon, but neither had ever put a person on the moon. *Apollo 11* was going to be the first manned spaceflight to land on the moon.

On July 16, 1969, *Apollo 11* launched and headed to the moon with three astronauts on board. Katherine had computed the path to get them there. The landing and successful return of *Apollo 11*'s flight to the moon made headlines all around the world. And it could not have been possible without Katherine's help.

Four days later, on July 20, 1969, Katherine, along with the rest of the world, watched on television as astronaut Neil Armstrong took mankind's first step on the moon. The little girl from White Sulphur Springs who loved to count had helped the US make world history! The US was now the clear leader in the Space Race.

Katherine admitted to being concerned about the return flight. "If we were off by just a few feet or seconds, they were done for," she remembered. "The astronauts wouldn't be able to return home."

Katherine had no need to worry. Her calculations were as accurate as ever. The astronauts splashed down safely in the Pacific Ocean on July 24, 1969.

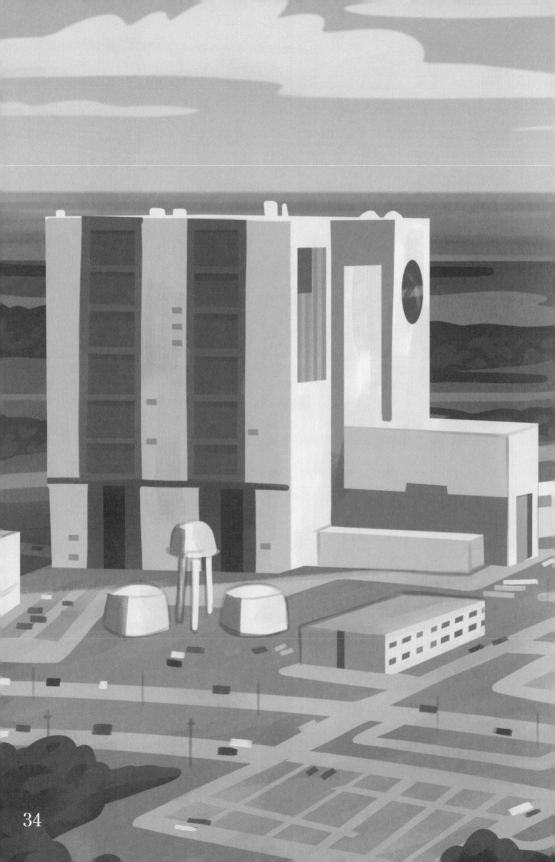

Chapter 5
An Infinite Contribution

Katherine worked on every space mission at NASA until she retired in 1986. She had done extraordinary, history-making work while raising her family, dealing with the death of her first husband in 1956, and getting remarried in 1959. "I found what I was looking for at NASA," said Katherine. "Never did I get up and say I don't want to go to work."

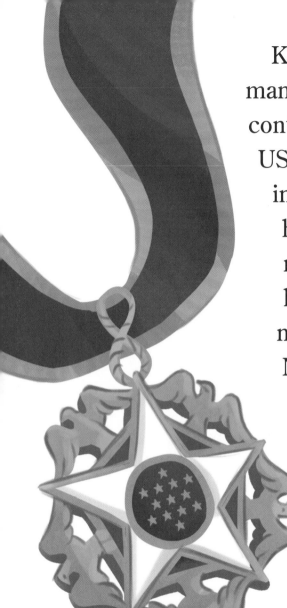

Katherine received many honors for her contribution to the US space program, including a flag that had gone to the moon. A building has also been named after her at NASA's Langley Research Center in Hampton, Virginia. In 2015 she received the Presidential Medal of Freedom. It is the highest honor an American civilian can receive. Katherine was ninety-seven at the time—an impressive number even for a math lover!

Katherine's love of math led her to help make history for the space program, for women's rights, and for racial equality. Through it all, Katherine remained humble about her remarkable achievements. She liked to quote her father, who used to tell her and her siblings, "You are as good as anybody. But you're no better."

Katherine shared her father's saying with the many students she spoke to after she retired. She wanted to encourage young people the way she had been encouraged. She also told them, "I like to learn. You can learn if you want to."

Now that you've met Katherine Johnson, don't *you* want to learn as much about your favorite subject as you can? Katherine is proof that if you stay grounded in what you love, the places you go can be out of this world!

BUT WAIT....

THERE'S MORE!

Turn the page to learn how sailors use the stars to guide them, some facts about outer space, and some cool careers that use math.

Star Power!

Long before Katherine helped humans travel to outer space, outer space helped humans travel the earth.

In ancient times most cultures kept land in sight when they sailed. It was a very slow way to travel across the ocean, but it helped keep ships from getting lost.

Over one thousand years ago Arab people found a way to sail straight across the Indian Ocean from one port to another. They used the North Star!

The North Star is a bright star in the handle of the constellation called the Little Dipper.

The North Star is special because it does not move across the sky. But if you travel north, the star appears to be higher in the sky. If you travel south, it appears to be lower.

Try it! Look across the room at something high on the wall, like a clock. As you walk toward the clock,

clock, you have to look up higher and higher to keep the clock in sight. The clock appears to be higher, just like the North Star.

To navigate, the Arab people created a tool called a kamal. In Arabic, "kamal" means "guide." It was a simple tool made of a wooden rectangle and a string. The kamal measured the height of the North Star. That told the sailors how far north they were.

If sailors knew how far north a port was, they could sail across the ocean directly to it. They simply sailed north or south from their home port until the kamal told them they were in the right spot.

With their ability to cross oceans, the Arab people traveled faster and more safely. They were able to trade with other cultures, earn money, and expand their territory.

Math Makes It Work!

From bakers to website makers, everyone uses math. But if you love solving problems, these awesome careers will add up to a lot of fun!

Want to create?

Engineers use math and science to help make almost anything you can think of!

Civil engineers plan out parts of cities and towns, like bridges, buildings, and sewers.

Mechanical engineers design mechanical engines, like those in cars, tools, and even toys!

Electrical engineers have a hand in designing electrical systems—from the ones found in smartphones to the power plants that keep the lights on in cities and towns.

Chemical engineers work with substances. They can help figure out how to make food taste better or to make fabric softer.

Aerospace engineers think up things that fly, like planes and helicopters.

Astronautical engineers are behind anything bound for outer space, like space shuttles and satellites.

Software engineers build worlds inside of computers. That's everything from the calculator on a smartphone to video games and virtual reality!

Want to discover?

These careers use math to collect information and make predictions.

Astronomers find new planets, stars, and so much more by watching and charting the night sky.

Meteorologists predict the weather using satellites, radar, and lots of cool tools.

Sports statisticians crunch numbers to tell newscasters and fans when a record has been set or an unlikely achievement has been made.

Music data journalists figure out which songs are popular, who might like which artists, and even what the next big hit will sound like.

These are just a few of the many jobs for people who love math!

Outer Space by the Numbers

- Our solar system has 1 star, 8 planets, 173 moons, and more than 3,400 comets and 715,000 asteroids. These numbers often change as we explore and make discoveries.

- The Earth's moon is about 238,855 miles away, or the length of 30 Earths sitting side by side.

- In our galaxy, the Milky Way, astronomers think there are between 100 and 400 billion stars, or maybe even more!

- *Voyager 1* became the 1st man-made object to leave our solar system.

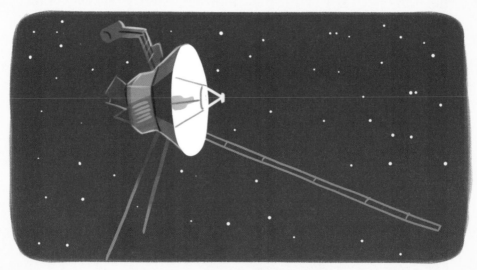

• *Voyager 1* and *2* launched in 1977 and have enough power to send information back to Earth until 2020—that's 43 years!

• Mars is, on average, 140 million miles from Earth.

• The temperature in outer space is -455 degrees Fahrenheit. That's more than 300 degrees colder than the coldest place on Earth, the South Pole!

• *Curiosity*, NASA's Mars rover, arrived on August 5, 2012, on Mars after a journey of 8 months. It is studying the planet's environment to find out if life is possible on Mars.

Now that you've met Katherine, what have you learned?

1. What did Katherine's father own?

a. farm   b. bank   c. store

2. When Katherine was little, what did most African American girls do after eighth grade?

a. go to ninth grade   b. learned to drive   c. help their families

3. What was Katherine's first job?

a. research mathematician   b. French teacher   c. physicist
                               and piano teacher

4. What country did the US compete with in the "Space Race"?

a. the Soviet Union   b. Canada   c. France

5. What did Katherine do for *Freedom 7*?

a. trained the astronauts   b. calculated the flight path   c. designed the rockets

6. What did Katherine help NASA achieve?

a. mankind's first step   b. the first American   c. both
   on the moon   orbiting earth

7. Before Katherine, how many women had been allowed to attend NASA briefing meetings?

a. none   b. one   c. ten

8. What did Katherine work on until 1986?

a. every NASA space   b. *Apollo 11*   c. Sputnik
   mission before she
   retired

9. Every morning before she retired, Katherine wanted to do what?

a. quit her job   b. earn recognition   c. go to work

10. According to Katherine, you can learn if what?

a. you're lucky   b. you want to   c. you know how

Answers: 1.a 2.c 3.b 4.a 5.b 6.c 7.a 8.a 9.c 10.b

REPRODUCIBLE